Master Your Mind, Master Your Business

Jules Beshears

Copyright © 2023 by Jules Beshears / 414 Industries

All rights reserved.

No portion of this book may be reproduced in any form without written permission from the publisher or author, except as permitted by U.S. copyright law.

Contents

Notes From The Author..1
Introduction 2
1. Introduction to 3
2. Understanding the Growth Mindset 8
3. Overcoming Limiting Beliefs and Negative Self-Talk................12
4. Building Resilience in the Face of Challenges and Failure..........15
5. Developing a Positive and Proactive Attitude 17
6. Time Management and Productivity for a Successful Mindset....20
7. Building and Maintaining a Supportive Network........................23
8. Effective Communication for Successful Business Relationships
....26
9. Managing Stress and Maintaining Work-Life Balance 29
10. Staying Focused and Motivated towards Your Goals 32
11. Mindset Strategies for Leadership and Team Building...............35
12. Conclusion and final thoughts on the importance of a strong business mindset. 38
414 Industries Online Courses...40

1.
2.
3.
4.
5.
6.
7.
8.
9.
10.
11.
12.
13.
14.

Notes From The Author

This book is a very distilled version of some of the mindset coaching I do. As such, you lose some of the personal stories. Instead, you are getting straight-to-the-point facts that have changed the lives of millions of people worldwide. My advice to the reader is to take notes or highlight this book. What I've found is that some parts resonate more with some people, and re-reading those sections routinely can really be a catalyst for change.

You may also feel as if some things are repeated. If they are, this is because we tend to remember and respond to things that are repeated. It's my solemn hope that this book and the learning within will drastically change your personal and professional life for the better.

This book is dedicated to my family and friends that stood by me when I was just starting and only had a dream.

Introduction

As an entrepreneur or business leader, you know that success is not just about having the right ideas or products. It's also about having the right mindset. Your thoughts and beliefs can either hold you back or propel you forward. They can impact your decision-making, motivation, and overall performance.

In this book, we'll explore the power of mindset in business and how you can use it to achieve your goals and reach new heights of success. You'll learn about the growth mindset, the impact of negative self-talk, the importance of resilience, and much more. We'll also provide practical strategies for building and maintaining a positive, productive, and successful mindset in the workplace.

Whether you're just starting in business or you're a seasoned entrepreneur, this book will provide you with the tools you need to develop and strengthen your business mindset. So get ready to take your thinking to the next level and discover the power of mindset in business.

Chapter one

Introduction to "The Power of Mindset in Business"

Success is often attributed to hard work, determination, and intelligent decision-making in today's business world. While these are undoubtedly important, the truth is that one's mindset can be just as crucial in determining success. Your mindset is your mental attitude and beliefs about yourself, others, and the world. It plays a critical role in shaping your behavior, emotions, and responses to challenges and opportunities in life and business.

The importance of mindset in business can be seen in the way it affects various aspects of your professional life, including:

1. Attitude towards challenges and failures: A growth mindset, characterized by a belief that abilities can be developed through effort and learning, allows individuals to approach challenges and failures as opportunities for growth, learning, and improvement. On the other hand, a fixed mindset, characterized by a belief that abilities cannot be changed, often leads to fear of failure and a lack of resilience in the face of challenges.
2. Confidence and self-esteem: A positive mindset can enhance an individual's confidence and self-esteem, allowing them to approach tasks and challenges with self-assurance. This can lead to better performance and tremendous success in business.

3. Decision-making: An individual's mindset can significantly influence how they make decisions and approach opportunities. A growth mindset can lead to a greater willingness to take risks, pursue new opportunities, and think creatively.
4. Relationships: A positive mindset can improve an individual's relationships with coworkers, customers, and partners. This can lead to better communication, more effective collaboration, and more robust professional networks.

The power of mindset should not be underestimated in the business world. By developing a growth mindset, individuals can unlock their full potential, overcome challenges, and achieve greater success. By adopting a positive, proactive, and confident outlook, individuals can transform their professional lives and create opportunities for growth and success in their careers.

Additionally, it's important to note that a growth mindset can be cultivated and developed. Here are a few steps that individuals can take to cultivate a growth mindset:

1. **Embrace challenges:** Rather than avoiding challenges, embrace them as opportunities for growth and learning. This will help you develop resilience and a sense of purpose in your work.
2. **Focus on progress, not perfection:** Rather than striving for perfection, focus on making progress and learning from your experiences. This will help you maintain a positive outlook and avoid becoming discouraged by setbacks.

3. **Surround yourself with positive influences:** Find individuals who have a growth mindset, support and encourage you, and challenge you to be your best.
4. **Reframe negative self-talk:** Rather than dwelling on negative thoughts and self-doubt, reframe them in a positive light. Focus on your strengths and abilities, and work to build your confidence and self-esteem.
5. **Embrace failure. It is a large part of the learning process:** Failure is natural and is part of the learning process. Embrace it as a way to learn and grow, and don't let it hold you back.

Incorporating these steps into your daily routine can help you cultivate a growth mindset and achieve tremendous business success. Remember, success is not just about working hard and making wise decisions but also about having the right mental attitude and approach. By developing a growth mindset, individuals can unlock their full potential and achieve their professional and personal goals.

Moreover, cultivating a growth mindset in an organization can also have a positive impact on company culture and success. Here are a few ways that organizations can encourage a growth mindset:

1. **Foster a culture of learning and development:** Encourage employees to continue learning and developing their skills through training and development opportunities. This helps employees feel valued and supported in their growth.
2. **Celebrate progress and effort, not just success:** Recognize and celebrate employee progress and effort, even if they haven't yet achieved their desired outcome. This reinforces a growth mindset and encourages employees to keep trying.

3. **Provide constructive feedback:** Provide feedback that is constructive, actionable, and focuses on areas for improvement. This helps employees feel supported and empowered to grow.
4. **Encourage risk-taking and experimentation:** Encourage employees to take risks and experiment with new ideas and approaches. This fosters a culture of innovation and creativity.
5. **Lead by example:** As a leader, demonstrate a growth mindset by embracing challenges, learning from failures, and continuously seeking growth and development. This sets a positive example for others in the organization.

By creating a culture that supports and encourages a growth mindset, organizations can foster a positive, resilient, and innovative workforce better equipped to navigate challenges and achieve success.

It's worth mentioning the role of mindfulness in developing a growth mindset. Mindfulness is the practice of bringing attention and awareness to the present moment. It helps individuals manage stress and emotions, improve focus, and develop a greater sense of self-awareness.

Here are a few ways that mindfulness can support a growth mindset:

1. **Improving emotional regulation:** Mindfulness can help individuals manage stress and emotions, allowing them to approach challenges with a clear and focused mind.
2. **Developing a positive outlook:** Mindfulness helps individuals develop a greater sense of gratitude and

appreciation, which can lead to a more positive outlook and greater happiness.
3. **Fostering self-awareness:** Mindfulness helps individuals become more self-aware, allowing them to understand their thoughts, beliefs, and behaviors and make positive changes as needed.
4. **Reducing self-criticism:** Mindfulness can help individuals reduce self-criticism and negative self-talk, which can undermine confidence and resilience.

By incorporating mindfulness into their daily routine, individuals can develop a growth mindset and achieve greater success in their professional and personal lives.

In conclusion, the power of mindset in business is immense. By developing a growth mindset, incorporating mindfulness, and creating a culture that supports growth and development, individuals and organizations can unlock their full potential and achieve success in their careers. The journey to success requires effort, determination, and the right mental approach. By prioritizing the development of a growth mindset, individuals and organizations can set themselves up for a brighter future.

Chapter two

Understanding the Growth Mindset

The growth mindset is a concept first popularized by psychologist Carol Dweck in her book, "Mindset: The New Psychology of Success." The growth mindset is the belief that intelligence, talent, and abilities can be developed through hard work, dedication, and learning. It is opposed to a fixed mindset, which is the belief that these traits are innate and cannot be changed.

Individuals with a growth mindset view challenges and failures as opportunities for growth and learning. In contrast, those with a fixed mindset often avoid challenges and see failures as evidence of their limitations. A growth mindset is crucial for success in life, as it encourages individuals to take risks, embrace challenges, and continuously learn and grow.

One of the key benefits of a growth mindset is that it allows individuals to persist in the face of adversity. When faced with a challenge, individuals with a growth mindset see it as an opportunity to learn and grow, while those with a fixed mindset may give up and view the challenge as a sign of their limitations.

Another benefit of a growth mindset is that it leads to greater motivation and engagement in work and personal pursuits. When individuals believe their abilities can be developed, they are more likely to embrace challenges and take an active role in their own learning and development.

It's worth noting that the growth mindset can be developed and cultivated over time. Here are a few steps that individuals can take to develop a growth mindset:

1. **Embrace challenges:** Rather than avoiding challenges, embrace them as opportunities for growth and learning. This will help you develop resilience and a sense of purpose in your work.
2. **Focus on progress, not perfection:** Rather than striving for perfection, focus on making progress and learning from your experiences. This will help you maintain a positive outlook and avoid becoming discouraged by setbacks.
3. **Surround yourself with positive influences:** Find individuals who have a growth mindset, who support and encourage you, and who challenge you to be your best.
4. **Reframe negative self-talk:** Rather than dwelling on negative thoughts and self-doubt, reframe them in a positive light. Focus on your strengths and abilities, and work to build your confidence and self-esteem.
5. **Embrace failure as part of the process:** Failure is ultimately an integral part of the learning process. Embrace it as a way to learn and grow, and don't let it hold you back.

By incorporating these steps into their daily routine, individuals can cultivate a growth mindset and achieve massive success in their personal and professional lives.

It is important to note that organizations can also adopt a growth mindset to drive success. By creating a culture that supports learning, development, and growth, organizations can foster a sense of purpose and motivation among employees. This can lead to increased productivity, innovation, and employee satisfaction.

Here are a few steps that organizations can take to develop a growth mindset:

1. **Encourage continuous learning:** Encourage employees to continuously learn and develop their skills through training, mentorship, and other development opportunities.
2. **Foster a culture of growth:** Create a culture that supports learning, development, and growth, where employees feel comfortable taking risks, embracing challenges, and learning from their mistakes.
3. **Provide opportunities for feedback:** Encourage employees to provide feedback to one another and provide opportunities for employees to receive constructive feedback from their managers. This can help individuals see their areas for improvement and work to develop their skills.
4. **Celebrate progress and success:** Celebrate progress and success, no matter how small, and recognize employees for their efforts and contributions.
5. **Lead by example:** Leaders should embody a growth mindset themselves, taking risks, embracing challenges, and continuously learning and growing. This will help set the tone for the rest of the organization.

By embracing a growth mindset, organizations can create a culture that supports learning, development, and growth, leading to increased productivity, innovation, and employee satisfaction.

In conclusion, the growth mindset is a powerful tool for success in both personal and professional contexts. By embracing challenges, focusing on progress, and surrounding themselves with positive influences, individuals can develop a growth mindset and achieve their personal and professional goals. Organizations can also adopt a growth mindset by creating a culture that supports learning, development, and growth, leading to increased productivity, innovation, and employee satisfaction.

Chapter three

Overcoming Limiting Beliefs and Negative Self-Talk

Limiting beliefs and negative self-talk can prevent individuals from achieving their full potential. These negative thoughts and beliefs can prevent individuals from pursuing their goals, taking risks, and stepping out of their comfort zones. However, with the right tools and strategies, individuals can overcome these limiting beliefs and negative self-talk and unlock their full potential.

Here are a few steps that individuals can take to overcome limiting beliefs and negative self-talk:

1. **Identify limiting beliefs:** Take time to reflect on the beliefs and thoughts holding you back. What negative thoughts do you have about yourself? What beliefs do you keep that limit your potential? Write them down and try to understand where they came from.
2. **Challenge limiting beliefs:** Once you've identified your limiting beliefs, challenge them. Ask yourself if they're true, and look for evidence to support or disprove them. This will help you gain a more accurate perspective on yourself and your abilities.
3. **Reframe negative self-talk:** Reframe negative self-talk in a more positive light. Rather than dwelling on negative thoughts and self-doubt, focus on your strengths and abilities. Surround

yourself with positive influences and work to build your confidence and self-esteem.
4. **Surround yourself with positive influences:** Individuals who have a growth mindset, who support and encourage you, and who challenge you to be your best.
5. **Focus on progress, not perfection:** Rather than striving for perfection, focus on making progress and learning from your experiences. This will help you maintain a positive outlook and avoid becoming discouraged by setbacks.
6. **Embrace failure:** Embrace failure as a natural part of the learning process. Don't let it hold you back; instead, view it as a learning experience.
7. **Practice self-compassion:** Treat yourself with kindness, understanding, and compassion. Don't be too hard on yourself; instead, focus on your efforts and progress.

If you begin incorporating these steps into your daily routine, individuals can overcome limiting beliefs and negative self-talk and unlock their full potential.

In conclusion, limiting beliefs and negative self-talk can prevent individuals from achieving their full potential. However, with the right tools and strategies, individuals can overcome these limiting beliefs and negative self-talk and unlock their full potential. Individuals can achieve their personal and professional goals by identifying limiting beliefs, reframing negative self-talk, surrounding themselves with positive influences, focusing on progress, embracing failure, and practicing self-compassion.

It's also important to recognize that overcoming limiting beliefs and negative self-talk is a journey and not a destination. It requires consistent effort and a willingness to be open to change.

One helpful tool in this journey is to practice mindfulness and self-reflection. This involves reflecting on your thoughts, feelings, and beliefs each day. Ask yourself questions like: What do I think about myself? How do I feel about myself? How are my beliefs impacting my actions?

Another helpful tool is to seek support from friends, family, or a therapist. Talking to someone about your limiting beliefs and negative self-talk can help you gain a new perspective and provide you with the support and encouragement you need to overcome them.

Finally, it's crucial to have a growth mindset and be open to learning and growing. This means being open to new experiences and perspectives, embracing challenges and failures, and continuously seeking to improve.

In summary, overcoming limiting beliefs and negative self-talk is a journey that requires consistent effort, self-reflection, support, and a growth mindset. By incorporating these tools and strategies into your daily routine, individuals can achieve their full potential and live a more fulfilling life.

Chapter four

Building Resilience in the Face of Challenges and Failure

Resilience is the ability to bounce back from challenges, failures, and setbacks. It's an essential trait for success in both personal and professional life, as challenges and failures are an inevitable part of the journey. Building resilience enables individuals to navigate challenges and failures with grace, determination, and a positive outlook.

Here are a few steps individuals can take to build resilience:

1. Embrace a growth mindset: Adopt a growth mindset, which views challenges and failures as opportunities to learn and grow. This mindset helps individuals maintain a positive outlook and focus on progress rather than perfection.
2. Cultivate a positive attitude: Focus on the positive aspects of challenges and failures. Seek out the lessons and opportunities they present, and maintain a positive attitude and outlook, even in the face of adversity.
3. Build strong relationships: Surround yourself with supportive and positive individuals who will encourage and motivate you through challenges and failures. Building solid relationships provide individuals with a network of support, which can help build resilience.
4. Take care of your physical and emotional well-being: Resilience is also built through taking care of oneself. This

means eating well, regularly exercising, and managing stress through mindfulness and meditation.
5. Learn from failures: Rather than viewing failures as setbacks, view them as opportunities to learn and grow. Reflect on your failures, and identify what you can learn from them to avoid making the same mistakes in the future.
6. Celebrate successes: Celebrate your successes, big and small, to build confidence and resilience. Recognizing your accomplishments helps you stay motivated and focused on your goals.
7. Develop a resilient identity: Develop a resilient identity by focusing on your strengths and abilities and embracing challenges as opportunities for growth. This helps you maintain a positive outlook, even in the face of adversity.

In conclusion, building resilience is essential for success in personal and professional life. By embracing a growth mindset, cultivating a positive attitude, building solid relationships, taking care of their physical and emotional well-being, learning from failures, celebrating successes, and developing a resilient identity, individuals can build resilience and navigate challenges and failures with grace and determination.

Chapter five

Developing a Positive and Proactive Attitude

Developing a Positive and Proactive Attitude

A positive and proactive attitude is crucial to personal and professional success. It helps individuals maintain a sense of hope and optimism, even in the face of challenges and failures. Developing a positive and proactive attitude requires a commitment to personal growth and a willingness to embrace change.

Here are a few steps individuals can take to develop a positive and proactive attitude:

1. **Embrace a growth mindset:** Adopt a growth mindset, which views challenges and failures as opportunities to learn and grow. This mindset helps individuals maintain a positive outlook and focus on progress rather than perfection.
2. **Cultivate gratitude:** Cultivate an attitude of gratitude by focusing on the positive areas of your life and expressing appreciation for what you have. This helps individuals maintain a positive outlook and a sense of hope.
3. **Surround yourself with positive individuals:** Surround yourself with positive, supportive individuals who will encourage and motivate you. Building strong relationships with positive individuals helps you maintain a positive outlook and a proactive attitude.

4. **Practice positive self-talk:** Replace negative self-talk with positive, empowering thoughts. Focus on your strengths and abilities, and maintain a positive outlook, even in the face of challenges and setbacks.
5. **Take action:** A proactive attitude requires taking action and being proactive in pursuing your goals and aspirations. Taking action helps individuals maintain a sense of control and a bold outlook.
6. **Focus on solutions:** Stop dwelling on problems and challenges; focus on finding solutions. This helps individuals maintain a positive outlook and a proactive attitude and enables them to find creative and effective solutions to challenges.
7. **Embrace change:** Embrace change as an opportunity for growth and personal development. A positive and proactive attitude requires a willingness to embrace change and continuously seek new and innovative solutions.

Individuals can also practice mindfulness and self-reflection to develop a positive and proactive attitude. Mindfulness involves being fully present in the moment and paying attention to one's thoughts, feelings, and surroundings. By practicing mindfulness, individuals can become more aware of their thought patterns and develop a greater sense of self-awareness.

Self-reflection is also vital for developing a positive and proactive attitude. This involves taking time to reflect on your thoughts, feelings, and experiences and identifying areas for growth and improvement. Self-reflection helps individuals better understand themselves and their motivations and enables them to cultivate a positive and proactive attitude.

In addition, individuals can also set achievable goals and take small steps toward their aspirations. This helps individuals maintain a sense of progress and momentum and contributes to a positive and proactive attitude.

Finally, it's important to maintain a healthy work-life balance to develop a positive and proactive attitude. This involves setting boundaries and taking time to rest, recharge, and pursue personal interests. A healthy work-life balance helps individuals maintain a sense of balance and perspective and contributes to a positive and proactive attitude.

In conclusion, developing a positive and proactive attitude requires embracing a growth mindset, cultivating gratitude, surrounding yourself with positive individuals, practicing positive self-talk, taking action, focusing on solutions, embracing change, practicing mindfulness and self-reflection, setting achievable goals, maintaining a healthy work-life balance. By incorporating these strategies into your daily routine, individuals can develop a positive and proactive attitude and achieve personal and professional goals.

Chapter six

Time Management and Productivity for a Successful Mindset

Time management and productivity are crucial components of a successful mindset. Effective time management helps individuals prioritize their tasks and responsibilities, while productivity enables individuals to make the most of their time and achieve their goals.

Here are a few tips for improving time management and productivity:

1. **Set clear goals:** Set clear, achievable goals for both the short-term and long-term. This helps individuals prioritize their tasks and responsibilities and maintain focus on what's important.
2. **Create a daily routine:** Establish a daily routine that includes time for work, rest, and leisure activities. A structured routine helps individuals prioritize their tasks and responsibilities and maintain a sense of balance and perspective.
3. **Use a to-do list:** Use a to-do list to keep track of tasks and responsibilities. Prioritize tasks based on importance and urgency, and regularly review and adjust your to-do list as necessary.
4. **Limit distractions:** Limit distractions, such as checking email or social media, to specific times during the day. This helps individuals maintain focus and prioritize their tasks and responsibilities.

5. **Learn to say "no":** Learning to say "no" is a crucial part of effective time management. Saying "no" to unimportant or unnecessary tasks helps individuals prioritize their responsibilities and focus on what's important.
6. **Take breaks:** Take breaks regularly to recharge and refresh. Regular breaks help individuals maintain focus, avoid burnout, and contribute to overall productivity.
7. **Delegate tasks:** Delegate tasks to others whenever possible. This helps individuals prioritize their tasks and responsibilities and frees up time for more important tasks.

Furthermore, it is also essential to be mindful of time-wasting activities and eliminate them. This could include activities such as excessive screen time, procrastination, and multitasking. Instead, focus on deep work, where you fully immerse yourself in one task at a time without distractions.

Additionally, incorporating healthy habits such as exercise, meditation, and proper sleep into your routine can also improve time management and productivity. These habits not only contribute to physical and mental well-being but also help individuals maintain a clear and focused mind, which is essential for successful time management and productivity.

It is also important to continually evaluate and adjust your time management and productivity strategies as needed. Regularly reflect on how you are using your time and make changes as necessary to ensure that you are making the most of your time and reaching your goals.

In conclusion, effective time management and productivity are crucial components of a successful mindset. By setting clear goals, creating a daily routine, using a to-do list, limiting distractions, learning to say "no," taking breaks, delegating tasks, eliminating time-wasting activities, incorporating healthy habits, and continually evaluating and adjusting your strategies, individuals can prioritize their duties and responsibilities, and make the most of their time to achieve their personal and professional goals and maintain a successful mindset.

Chapter seven

Building and Maintaining a Supportive Network

Having a supportive network of friends, family, and colleagues is crucial for maintaining a successful mindset. A supportive network provides individuals with encouragement, motivation, and a sense of belonging, which are essential for personal and professional growth.

Here are a few tips for building and maintaining a supportive network:

1. **Cultivate existing relationships:** Invest time and effort into maintaining existing relationships with friends, family, and colleagues. Regularly communicate, share experiences, and offer support to strengthen these relationships.
2. **Attend networking events:** Attend networking events to meet new people and expand your network. Look for events related to your interests and professional goals, and be open to making new connections.
3. **Volunteer:** Volunteer for causes or organizations that align with your values and interests. Volunteering is a great way to meet like-minded individuals and make new connections.
4. **Join a professional organization:** Join a professional organization related to your field of work. This is a great way to connect with others in your industry and expand your network.

5. **Connect with mentors:** Connect with individuals who can serve as mentors. Mentors can provide guidance, advice, and support and can play a crucial role in personal and professional growth.
6. **Stay in touch:** Regularly stay in touch with members of your network. This helps to maintain relationships and keep your network strong and supportive.
7. **Offer support:** Offer support and encouragement to members of your network. Supporting others helps to build strong relationships and strengthens your network.

Moreover, it is important to have a support system within the workplace. This can involve positive relationships with coworkers, seeking guidance and mentorship from superiors, and having a supportive work culture that encourages growth and development.

A supportive work environment not only boosts morale and job satisfaction but can also lead to better job performance, increased productivity, and a reduced risk of burnout. Additionally, having a supportive network within the workplace can also provide individuals with opportunities for professional growth and advancement.

In order to build and maintain a supportive network, it is also important to communicate openly and effectively. Good communication skills can help to build trust, foster positive relationships, and resolve conflicts in a productive manner.

It is also essential to be intentional about the relationships you form and maintain. Seek out individuals who have similar values, interests, and goals, and be open to developing connections with others. Being intentional about your relationships can help to build a network that is supportive and fulfilling.

In conclusion, building and maintaining a supportive network is an essential aspect of a successful mindset. A supportive network provides individuals with encouragement, motivation, and a sense of belonging and is crucial for personal and professional growth. By cultivating existing relationships, attending networking events, volunteering, joining a professional organization, connecting with mentors, staying in touch, offering support, having a supportive work environment, and communicating effectively, individuals can build and maintain a robust and supportive network that contributes to their success and well-being.

Chapter eight

Effective Communication for Successful Business Relationships

Effective communication is essential for building and maintaining successful business relationships. Good communication skills can help to build trust, foster positive relationships, and resolve conflicts in a productive manner.

Here are a few tips for effective communication in business relationships:

1. **Listen actively:** Make an effort to truly listen to what the other person is saying and avoid interrupting. Active listening shows that you respect the other person's perspective and value their input.
2. **Be clear and concise:** When communicating, be clear and concise in your message. Avoid using complex language or technical terms that may be confusing to others.
3. **Use nonverbal cues:** Nonverbal cues such as body language, facial expressions, and tone of voice can play a significant role in communication. Be aware of your nonverbal cues and make sure they align with the message you are trying to convey.
4. **Ask questions:** Ask questions to clarify information and gain a better understanding of the other person's perspective. This can help to build rapport and foster positive relationships.

5. **Stay calm and professional:** When communicating, it is essential to stay calm and professional, even in tense or stressful situations. This can help to de-escalate conflicts and maintain positive relationships.
6. **Provide feedback:** Provide regular feedback to others to help improve communication and resolve conflicts. Be specific and constructive in your feedback, and focus on solutions rather than blaming others.
7. **Use empathy:** Try to understand the other person's perspective and show compassion. This can help to build trust and foster positive relationships.

Additionally, it is important to consider cultural differences when communicating in business. Different cultures may have different norms and expectations for communication, and it is crucial to be aware of these differences to avoid misunderstandings.

Effective communication also involves being open and transparent. Be honest and upfront about your intentions, goals, and expectations, and encourage others to do the same. This can help to build trust and foster positive relationships.

In order to improve your communication skills, it is also important to continually seek out opportunities for growth and development. This may involve taking courses or workshops, seeking feedback from others, practicing active listening and speaking, and learning from past experiences.

Furthermore, technology has dramatically impacted the way we communicate in business. Email, instant messaging, and video conferencing have become standard methods of communication in the workplace. It is essential to be proficient in using these technologies and in understanding the etiquette and norms for communication in these digital platforms.

In conclusion, effective communication is an essential aspect of successful business relationships. By being aware of cultural differences, being open and transparent, continually seeking opportunities for growth, and being proficient in technology, individuals can improve their communication skills and build strong, positive business relationships.

Chapter nine

Managing Stress and Maintaining Work-Life Balance

Stress and burnout are common challenges faced by many individuals in the workplace and can negatively impact both personal and professional life. Maintaining a healthy work-life balance is crucial for reducing stress and promoting overall well-being.

Here are a few tips for managing stress and maintaining work-life balance:

1. **Set boundaries:** Set clear boundaries between work and personal time to avoid overworking and burnout. This may involve establishing a regular schedule, limiting after-hours work, and taking breaks throughout the day.
2. **Prioritize self-care:** Take time to engage in activities that promote physical and mental well-being, such as exercise, meditation, and hobbies.
3. **Stay organized:** Develop effective time management and organizational skills to reduce stress and increase productivity. This may involve using to-do lists, prioritizing tasks, and delegating responsibilities.
4. **Maintain a positive attitude:** Cultivate a positive attitude and focus on solutions rather than dwelling on problems. This can help to reduce stress and maintain a healthy work-life balance.

5. **Foster supportive relationships:** Surround yourself with positive, supportive individuals who can offer encouragement and motivation. This can help to reduce stress and maintain a healthy work-life balance.
6. **Practice stress-management techniques:** Engage in stress-management techniques such as deep breathing, progressive muscle relaxation, and mindfulness.
7. **Seek support:** Seek support from a therapist, counselor, or support group if needed. This can help to manage stress and maintain a healthy work-life balance.

Additionally, it's important to recognize the signs of burnout and seek help if needed. Some common symptoms of burnout include feeling physically and emotionally exhausted, having decreased motivation and satisfaction, and experiencing a decrease in work performance.

It's also important to understand that work-life balance may look different for each individual, and there is no one-size-fits-all approach. Some people may prioritize work and prioritize their careers, while others may prioritize their personal life and relationships. Finding a balance that works for you is key.

In the workplace, employers can play a role in promoting work-life balance for their employees. This may involve offering flexible work arrangements, providing opportunities for professional development and growth, and promoting a positive work environment.

Overall, maintaining a healthy work-life balance requires effort and a commitment to self-care. By being mindful of stress levels, seeking support when needed, and taking steps to promote overall well-being, individuals can achieve success both in their personal and professional lives.

Managing stress and maintaining a healthy work-life balance is crucial for promoting overall well-being and success in both personal and professional life. By setting boundaries, prioritizing self-care, staying organized, maintaining a positive attitude, fostering supportive relationships, practicing stress-management techniques, and seeking support when needed, individuals can reduce stress and promote a healthy work-life balance.

Chapter ten

Staying Focused and Motivated towards Your Goals

Staying focused and motivated toward your goals is crucial for success in both your personal and professional life. Here are a few tips for staying focused and motivated:

1. **Set clear, specific, and achievable goals:** Identify what you want to achieve, and break down larger goals into smaller, manageable tasks. This can help to increase motivation and focus.
2. **Create a plan:** Develop a plan of action to achieve your goals, including specific steps and a timeline. This can help to keep you focused and on track.
3. **Stay accountable:** Hold yourself accountable for your actions and progress towards your goals. Consider working with a coach, mentor, or accountability partner to help keep you focused and motivated.
4. **Celebrate your successes:** Take time to celebrate your achievements and accomplishments, no matter how small. This can help to increase motivation and sustain focus toward your goals.
5. **Stay positive:** Maintain a positive attitude and focus on solutions rather than dwelling on problems. This can help to increase motivation and sustain focus toward your goals.

6. **Surround yourself with positive influences:** Surround yourself with individuals who support and encourage you and who share your values and goals.
7. **Stay motivated:** Keep yourself motivated by regularly reviewing your progress and renewing your commitment to your goals. Consider setting new, challenging goals to continue growing and developing.

Staying focused and motivated toward your goals requires a combination of planning, self-awareness, and a commitment to personal growth. By setting clear, specific, and achievable goals, creating a plan, staying accountable, celebrating successes, staying positive, surrounding yourself with positive influences, and staying motivated, individuals can achieve their goals and succeed in both their personal and professional life.

It's important to understand that motivation can fluctuate, and it's okay to have moments of doubt or feeling discouraged. Here are a few tips for maintaining motivation when faced with challenges:

1. **Reframe negative thoughts:** Do not dwell on negative thoughts and self-doubt. Try to reframe them into a positive and proactive perspective. This can help to increase motivation and maintain focus towards your goals.
2. **Stay focused on your why:** Remind yourself of the reasons why you set your goals in the first place and the benefits of achieving them. This can help to increase motivation and sustain focus towards your goals.
3. **Embrace failure:** Embrace failure as an opportunity for growth and learning. Instead of viewing failure as a setback,

view it as a stepping stone towards success. This can help to increase motivation and maintain focus towards your goals.
4. **Stay organized:** Stay organized by prioritizing tasks and keeping track of progress towards your goals. This can help to increase motivation and maintain focus towards your goals.
5. **Take care of yourself:** Take care of your physical, emotional, and mental well-being. This can help to increase motivation and maintain focus towards your goals.
6. **Stay open-minded:** Stay open-minded and willing to embrace change and new opportunities. This can help to increase motivation and maintain focus towards your goals.

In conclusion, maintaining motivation and focus towards your goals requires a combination of self-awareness, positive thinking, and a commitment to personal growth. By reframing negative thoughts, staying focused on your why, embracing failure, staying organized, taking care of yourself, and staying open-minded, individuals can increase motivation and achieve their goals.

Chapter eleven

Mindset Strategies for Leadership and Team Building

Leadership and team building are critical components of success in business. Here are a few mindset strategies for leadership and team building:

1. **Lead by example:** Lead by example by demonstrating the behaviors and attitudes you expect from your team. This can help to build trust, increase motivation, and create a positive and supportive work environment.
2. **Empower and encourage:** Empower and motivate your team members by providing them with the resources, support, and autonomy they need to succeed. This can help to increase motivation and build a strong, collaborative team.
3. **Foster open communication:** Foster open communication by actively seeking feedback, encouraging open dialogue, and promoting transparency. This can help to build trust and increase collaboration among team members.
4. **Celebrate successes:** Celebrate the achievements of your team, both big and small. This can help to increase motivation and build a positive and supportive work environment.
5. **Embrace diversity:** Embrace diversity by valuing the unique perspectives and experiences of each team member. This can help to build a strong, collaborative team and drive innovation.

6. **Encourage personal and professional growth:** Encourage personal and professional growth by providing opportunities for training, development, and advancement. This can help to increase motivation and build a solid and collaborative team.
7. **Model a growth mindset:** Model a growth mindset by embracing challenges, learning from failures, and promoting a positive and proactive attitude. This can help to increase motivation and build a positive and supportive work environment.

It is important to remember that leadership and team building is an ongoing process that requires continuous effort and attention. Here are a few additional strategies for leadership and team building:

1. **Encourage teamwork:** Encourage teamwork by promoting collaboration and cooperation among team members. This can help to build a strong, cohesive team that is better able to work together towards common goals.
2. **Promote accountability:** Promote accountability by setting clear expectations and holding team members accountable for their actions. This can help to build a strong, productive team that is better able to achieve its goals.
3. **Encourage innovation:** Encourage innovation by promoting creativity, encouraging risk-taking, and valuing new ideas and approaches. This can help to drive innovation and build a solid and forward-thinking team.
4. **Provide regular feedback:** Provide regular feedback to team members, both positive and constructive, to help them understand their strengths and areas for improvement. This

can help to increase motivation, build trust, and foster personal and professional growth.
5. **Promote a positive work environment:** Promote a positive work environment by valuing teamwork, encouraging collaboration, and promoting a supportive and inclusive culture. This can help to increase motivation, build trust, and foster a strong, productive team.
6. **Lead with empathy:** Lead with empathy by understanding the needs and perspectives of your team members. This can help to build trust, increase motivation, and foster a positive and supportive work environment.

Effective leadership and team building require a combination of self-awareness, positive thinking, and a commitment to personal and professional growth. By encouraging teamwork, promoting accountability, encouraging innovation, providing regular feedback, promoting a positive work environment, and leading with empathy, leaders can build strong, motivated, and productive teams that drive success in business.

Chapter twelve

Conclusion and final thoughts on the importance of a strong business mindset.

In conclusion, the power of mindset in business cannot be overstated. A strong business mindset is essential for success in today's fast-paced, competitive business world. By understanding the growth mindset, overcoming limiting beliefs and negative self-talk, building resilience, developing a positive and proactive attitude, managing time effectively, building and maintaining a supportive network, communicating effectively, managing stress and maintaining work-life balance, staying focused and motivated, and using effective leadership and team-building strategies, individuals can cultivate a strong business mindset that drives success and fulfillment in both their personal and professional lives.

In closing, it's important to remember that a strong business mindset is a valuable asset that can help you to achieve your goals and reach new levels of success in your career. Whether you are just starting out in business or are a seasoned professional, investing in your mindset can have a profound impact on your personal and professional growth and success. So start taking control of your mindset today, and take your business to new heights of success and fulfillment!

It's also important to keep in mind that a strong business mindset is not just about achieving success and prosperity but also about finding fulfillment and happiness in your personal and professional life. By embracing a growth mindset, developing resilience, building positive relationships, and cultivating a positive attitude, you can find greater joy and satisfaction in your work and in your life as a whole.

Additionally, it's important to remember that a strong business mindset is not just a personal attribute but also a valuable asset to the organizations you work with. By fostering a positive and proactive attitude, you can bring positive energy, creativity, and a collaborative spirit to your workplace and help to build a culture of success and growth.

In conclusion, the importance of a strong business mindset cannot be overstated. By embracing a growth mindset, overcoming limiting beliefs and negative self-talk, building resilience, developing a positive and proactive attitude, managing time effectively, building and maintaining a supportive network, communicating effectively, managing stress and maintaining work-life balance, staying focused and motivated, and using effective leadership and team-building strategies, individuals can cultivate a strong business mindset that drives success, fulfillment, and happiness in both their personal and professional lives. So start investing in your mindset today, and see the positive impact it can have on your life and career!

414 Industries Online Courses

We never stop learning. Check out other books by Jules Beshears and 414 Industries

https://amzn.to/3xib4Ph Checkout our books on amazon

https://414industries.com/

https://www.instagram.com/414industries/

https://www.facebook.com/414industries

www.ingramcontent.com/pod-product-compliance
Lightning Source LLC
Chambersburg PA
CBHW050241220526
45465CB00017B/834